Puppet

Poems by Ben Rasnic

ISBN-13:978-0615752945

Cover photograph by Beatrice Murch
http://www.flickr.com/photos/blmurch/375719425/

Alabaster Leaves Publishing
1840 West 220th Street, Suite 300
Torrance, California 90501

Acknowledgements

"Walking at Night in Our Nation's Capital" and "The Absolution of July" originally appeared in *Short, Fast and Deadly.*

"African Cichlids" originally appeared in *Indigo Rising.*

"My Father's Family Portrait" originally appeared in *A Small Good Magazine.*

"The Carnival" originally appeared in *Asphodel Madness.*

"Finding Place", "The Cremation", "Cinnabar", "Light and Dark: The Sleeping Forest", "Rendezvous" and "Role Models" first appeared in *Jimson Weed.*

"Of Hillbillies, Hobos & Poets", "Just before Leaving" and "Of Kuhlken" originally appeared in *The Dead Mule.*

"Bully" and "BP" originally appeared in *Eunoia Review.*

"2011 Dog", "Occupied", "Old Photographs Stare like Death" and "Popcorn Anyone?" first appeared in *The Rusty Truck.*

"What Lies Between the Lines" first appeared in *Subliminal Interiors.*

"Monopoly" originally appeared in *Puffin Circus.*

"Snow Blind", "Puppet" and "Scenes from an Earlier Life" originally appeared in *Ink, Sweat & Tears.*

"Strange Day" and "Metamorphosis" originally appeared in *Gutter Eloquence.*

"October" originally appeared in *Quantum Poetry Magazine.*

"Insomnia" and "Toys in the Attic" first appeared in *Foliate Oak.*

"Harlan County Blues", "Popeye" and "Still Life from a High School Parking Lot" originally appeared in *The Orange Room Review.*

"The Crow" first appeared in *Chickenpinata.*

"Small Town Friday Nights in September" originally appeared in *Flutter Magazine.*

"Night Sounds (Appalachia, VA)" and "Snowglobe" originally appeared in *Word Catalyst.*

"Scottsboro 9", "Watching the Men Lay Cable through the Neighborhood" and "Life" first appeared in *Eskimo Pie.*

"Ti Jean", "Take as Directed" and "Spinning" originally appeared in *Blue & Yellow Dog.*
"Hope" originally appeared in *Gloom Cupboard.*
"Mirage (Nevada Moon)" first appeared in *The Camel Saloon.*
"Last Dance" originally appeared in *Thirteen Myna Birds.*
"Big Stone Gap, The Early Years" and "Fishing Wallen's Creek originally appeared in *The Clinch Mountain Review.*
"Windowpane" originally appeared in *Calliope Nerve.*
"Homage to Mr. Wizard" and "May 9, 2010" originally appeared in *Red River Review.*
"Stick Horse" originally appeared in *Westward Quarterly.*
"The Eleventh Month" originally appeared in *Jellyfish Whispers.*

Table of Contents

Walking at Night in Our Nation's Capital

Another evening spent
walking along the outer perimeter
of police tape
sucking the yellow
out of a full moon.

African Cichlids

They swim with the indigenous ease
of hot butter skating
across flashing table knives,
like fallen flowers
laced in a steady current
of alkaline rain.

Beneath fluorescent moon
of simulated lake menagerie,
the riff of fluent brush strokes swirl
from watercolor palettes
of bullet shaped streamlined bodies
bred for speed & grace;

The flare of finned wings glides
and swoops the lucidity of charcoal filtered waves,
sometimes content in simply hovering
like string puppets yet territorial
by nature, sometimes darting in an instant
at the scent of a fight

or twitching
from androgynous love,
whipping like an egg beater
in a scream of pigments,
whippoorwilling their kodachrome
over white coral.

Angling through pockets
of artificial rock formations,
caves and plastic plants;
performing ritual dances

of African lake ancestors;
at times you can catch them

relaxed & content,
transcending into an integral part
of our domestic lives;

hooked on high def digital cable,
nightlight
for the grandkids………..

My Father's Family Portrait

It could have been
the cover for Steinbeck's
"Grapes of Wrath"

Late 1930's,
composed in black & white
for a black and white world--

Hitler annihilating the Jews,
Louis pummeling Schmelling,
The dark divide of the Great Depression.

Almost everyone in the photo
dressed in their Sunday best
despite hard times indelibly etched
into stone faces.

It is a sunny day
as everyone is squinting, forcing
an obliged look of tolerance,

My father is the one in the back row
with the trademark snarl
like Sean Penn from a previous life.

I imagine him mumbling
under his breath something like
"Burning daylight, got chores to do."

The only person smiling
is the youngest, yet she too
will come to experience

the burden the weight of the world
can have on the shoulders
of its children

as they struggle with the earth
& its elements
for their daily bread

only to be left at the end of the day
on a dead-end country road, forcing
an obliged look of tolerance.

The Carnival

August heat precipitates
steady rain feathering
pink cotton candy swirls
and watercolor canvas pools
wavering in neon funhouse mirrors.

Sideshow games tilt
from leaded milk bottles
and greased crystal dishes,
shooting gallery rifles with bent sights
and barrels crooked as a raccoon's penis.

Bearded bikers
sport tattered denim,
arms plastered
in purple ink tattoos
man the ride controls.

We ride the Scrambler, the Cyclops,
the Tilt-a-Whirl and finally,
the Ferris Wheel where we kiss
until our lips chap, then cozy up
in the black curtained booth,

my sweaty palms pressed
against her bare naked breasts
for the first time,
nipples pink and swelling
like candied apples;

exit through a mud puddle maze,
                    ghost image film strips
of blurred lives
and spent quarters
trampled underfoot.

Of Hillbillies, Hobos & Poets

Following the beaten dirt path
past dilapidated barns
with wood planks gapped
like missing teeth;

down by the creek
where campfire flames lick
blackened cans
of pork & beans;

they take refuge
in the east Tennessee
summer night--

a myriad of voices
exchanging stories
over shish-kabobbed catfish
on nylon stringers.

Finding Place

Without shelter,
you find your place
among the sleeping trees
in woods of your own nature.

Let rest your tired,
old bones— park bench
among the artifacts
& brittle leaves.

A few sparrows come to greet you,
hopping hungrily at your feet,
mulching the bread crumbs you left them
from the lunch in yr brown paper sack.

You tell them stories & they listen—
a smile in yr white beard
for things having lost
their usefulness.

just before leaving

these days
gray cloud cover
looms
over Appalachian
mountains
once a homespun quilt
to blanket
my insecurity
shrouds me
now
an angler's seine
to snare
stray fish;
a black widow's
cruel artistry
to secure
my foolishness
as to think
that simple
geography
could hold me
like a
lover.

Of Kuhlken

Stopped in for a few
beers at some
outoftheway saloon
north of Cheyenne,
neon flickering
a crosswind
hurling tumbleweed.

Trail dust fever—
rode that Pontiac
all the way from Virginia
without a hitch,
two weary soul mates
in search of
a new frontier

Crossed the Dakotas, dreamscape
of the Badlands—tracked sand dunes
for artifacts, teeth of arrows
scoring hard evidence of Indian
blood ties, legends of grandfathers
excavating their magic, secrets
from the skulls of geology,
essence of mind spirit.

Camped for hours
without the benefit
of peyote, witnessed
a fleeting glimpse
of cavalry brigade retreating
from the leaping flames

and the strange gray passage
of time dispersing into
distant mist of horizon.

Coyote nearby,
siren breaking the fortress
of silence,
worshipping the new moon,
pissing on dry prairie……….

You passed thru
the swinging wood doors
grinning like a Cheshire cat,
a modern day Billy the Kid
in Muddy Waters clothing.

Cinnabar

is her name
styled from the novella
by Ed Bryant,
but I call her
kitty,   sometimes
fur-balled malcontent,
either reference
she responds to;

wheat hair textured
like barbed wire fleecing
the rust of a desert wind;

goes about her business
undaunted by world events,
tears into comic strips
easeled by comfortable laps,
perfecting Garfield imitations.

Half her life spent sleeping
in the bay window seat
among the half-chewed African Violets
and the shredded ivy, coiled and yawning
like a python,

the other half
on the prowl, skeet shooting
at traces of food, water,
sometimes affection,

endless aerobics
of paw pads tattooing
the flesh
of indulging humans;

times her leaps
with bionic precision

a mercuric fluid style
indecisive at doorways.

Bully

Some of them carried pocket knives,
cruised the neighborhoods posturing
for a fight; tortured small animals
for kicks.

One would flash me the peace sign
then ram his fingertips between my ribs;
leave me sprawled on the ground, helpless,
gasping for air.

Called me "sissy" and "mama's boy"
for not sticking frogs
or blasting birds out of the sky
with a twelve gauge scattergun;

Broke my nose for not taking a turn
pounding the spinster neighbor's housecat
into the pavement with the blunt end
of a Louisville Slugger.

The awareness that a jury of his peers
would someday sentence him to ten
of his adult years in federal prison
would have appreciably anesthetized my pain..........

During the summers I walked for miles
to his parent's mansion on the hill
towing my Murray 16-inch push mower

before the days of self propelled
when $10 for only 4 hours hard labor
was an offer too lucrative to let pass

even when it meant
not going fishing with my buddies
or missing the Bronx Bombers
on the black & white ;

even when it meant
ice cold water sprayed down my back
every time I staggered to the back door
to collect my pay

and his shrill laughter
would ring in my ears
like the penetrating shriek
of a frightened little girl

or a helpless victim
before the testosterone rage
of misguided young men.

2011 Dog

(after reading Ferlinghetti's "Dog")

The dog no longer trots
freely down the street
but in a smothering choke hold
from his master's leather leash.

And what he sees
are not the things
he was bred to see,
riding in cars rather than chasing,
strapped into a safety harness, slobbering
on the upholstery & power windows.

The dog no longer trots
freely down the street
and what he sees
are not the things he was bred to see--

caged kennels
with concrete walkways,
high maintenance pooches
with matching sweaters and caps.

No longer does he explore
whatever avenues his nose points him toward;
no longer does he exude
the pronounced swagger of his forefathers
on the prowl for a piece of tail
down some seedy alleyway.

And if he barks at the moon,
they will camouflage barbiturates
in his doggy chow
or surgically remove his larynx
to comply with local nuisance laws.

Now he must endure
with shame and disgrace,
the image of his master on all fours
with metal scoop and plastic bag
to remove his once proud
public excretions.

And he must be thinking to himself
what other free thinkers
are thinking,
"What has happened to my America?"

and to those who prefer
to walk these streets with blinders on,
the dog raises his flea infested
left hind leg
in salute.

Occupied

We scrub our minds clean
as blank scrabble tiles,
attune our senses
to the numbing drone
of throbbing, repetitive drum beats.

Grunts and squeals can still be heard
emanating from the gilded canyons
of Wall Street
with each ticker tape fluctuation.

In the name of freedom
we have sacrificed our individuality,
vocabularies reduced
to hand lettered cardboard placards,
unsophisticated hand signals
& mic check chants

apparently oblivious to the inevitable truth
that change is just another name
for more of the same;
that whenever power changes hands,
the pigs will still be running the farm.

What Lies Between the Lines

When the giddy,
fresh from grad school teacher
proudly beamed to her students
"You can be anything you want to be,
including President!"
she failed to mention
the obvious consequences
such as the steady progression
of flag draped caskets
or the easily acquired
demeanor of deceit,
upon auctioning off
one's borrowed soul.

Monopoly

was either the car or the dog, at times
the wheelbarrow, always something with wheels
or feet to maneuver around the board
pass GO and collect $200

but a hat? an iron? a thimble?
had Parker Brothers merged with Doobie Brothers?
no matter as every game played out the same always
broke by midnight playing against my brothers

the three of us in matching plaid pajamas
wired on ice cream floats, Oreo cookies
and coca-colas whenever the snow would sock us in
"No school tomorrow" meant Monopoly Marathon;

shake rattle and roll the dice
take a chance card and
a ride on the Reading
or open up Community Chest & find
a Get out of Jail Free card

I was always The Slumlord of the Purple Squares,
Baltic and Mediterranean
the estates of my Fiefdom;
sometimes proclaiming myself the King of Marvin Gardens

but Park Place and Boardwalk
were never in the cards
except to land there at my brother's hotel
and lose everything
and that's the way it always was

and now finding myself
down on my luck
this comes to mind—

seems the die has been cast
and I'm out of the game;

flat broke
without even a thimble
to my name.

Snow Blind

In early April
an arctic storm
is spilling snowflakes.

She peels away the sheets
and slips toward the kitchen;
silk robe gliding
gently to the floor.

The tea kettle screams
with hot wet steam;
ceramic coffee cups spiked
with Morning Thunder and cinnamon sticks.

I wipe the windowpane fog,
watch seagulls wing thru crystal mist.

Neighbors busy with shovels,
carpool for groceries;
tire tracks tattooing the glazed asphalt.

Rust colored snowplow scrapes like a razor blade
tapering white granular lines
across a glass tabletop.

The world keeps spinning its wheels
while we patiently explore
the familiar contours of flesh and bone.

Snow blind, I bury my face
in the crest of her thighs,
her fingernails carving slaloms
down the slope of my back.

Soft plush
of thick white down
swells beyond our horizons;

white powder
consuming the landscape;
consuming everything.

Scenes from an Earlier Life

(Lee Theater, Pennington Gap, Va.)

Before sealing its doors in '78
it was THE place to be Saturday nights,
line forming from the ticket booth stretching
down Morgan Avenue, flexed and undulating
like a human centipede;
where checking out who was there with whom
and sometimes who was not there with whom
but with someone else
actually provided more entertainment
than the library of Elvis Presley flicks
and spaghetti westerns we had come to view.

And once inside, would breathe in
that familiar smell, the unmistakable marriage
of English Leather cologne and mildew
challenging the senses
as well as the stale but sweet mask
of hot buttered popcorn and licorice sticks
always waiting there for us
like the bubble gum & Bit-o-Honeys
stuck to the underside of upholstered cushion seats.

Yet when the majestic velvet curtain
would at long last draw open
to unveil the mammoth canvas screen
to the creaking whir of projector,
the chill bumps on my arms could not be denied
as reels and reels of spliced, grainy film
played out their final respective shelf lives

while real life was being played out
in the balcony atop the carpeted stairwell
that spiraled back in time to Jim Crow,
now occupied by naïve white adolescents
fumbling with buttons, clasps and zippers;

nervous whispers and heavy breathing
scoring raw footage from unfinished lives
permanently archived in the flickering light.

Strange Day

I sometimes wonder
Mr. Mojo Risin,
did you finally find
what you were looking for

that strange Parisian day
your alcohol ravaged soul bargained
with the angels
to break on through
to the other side?

October

The breeze attending
this afternoon's drizzle
contains a certain chill.

Behind a misty veil,
sun softens its vigilant eye
as, at the edge of town,
the crowd in the stadium
has turned, like rotting fruit.

Soon, clouds of smoke
from the orange skulls
of flaming pumpkins
will mask a full yellow moon

and the crisp night air
will succumb
to the chants
of tiny extortionists.

Insomnia

Late night television flickers classic
cinematic apparitions across white walls
framing Ansel Adams prints;
a black & white world
where color is reserved for dreams.

Moth wings motor whirling drumsticks
against the taut window screen.
Egyptian cat clock trickles an echo, measures
syncopation of time
in Chinese water torture..................

Wood floors curiously creak
without footsteps.
I can feel the room breathing;
becoming my own halting breath.

Abruptly, the old Frigidaire reboots
with the whirring of an old laptop
or a hissing serpent
winding through copper tubing.

Electric wiring hums through drywall,
pulses through my veins,
extending frayed nerve endings.

Train horn flares its nostrils, wails
like a coyote
as Norfolk Southern winds down
before the railway crossing

Light and shadows alternate
like a pendulum or a metronome
measuring time like a beating heart
as I lie in stillness
with dreams of sleep.

Harlan County Blues

the Lord gave and the Lord hath taken away'

Job 1:20-21

Houses on stilts perch precariously
from sloped hillsides—heirlooms
of poverty passed
from generation to generation
destined to back roads unraveling
detours to dead ends.

Scar tissue tattoos
what Autumn once admired—
panoramic ridge of saffron, crimson
and goldenrod lay stretched below,
far as the eye could see.

Now shiny yellow D10 dozers rumble
in the mountain mist; armored tanks
trudge laboriously through the black mud.
Once cool crystal springs occupied with trout
now spill into stagnant sludge ponds,
all in the name of cheap coal..................

Old man slouches on his sagging porch swing
& whittles a cedar stick; lungs wheezing
Like a dangled accordion; diminishing flicker
of moth wings in his eyes.
Cattle stand almost vertically
with astonished blank stares,
grazing without pasture.

Laundry hangs linear
from 12 gauge wire
nailed to wooden crosses,
sways in the breeze

like pennants
at a used car lot

as scruffy faced children
sit on boulders
playing cat's cradle—

coal dust under their feet
and stardust in their eyes.

Popeye

My father was a hard man,
even his countenance gave the appearance
of lines and crevices chiseled in granite.

Any semblance of backtalk
was typically greeted with a stone fist
flush on the face;

his brick solid biceps & sinewy forearms
dark brown from southern exposure
and an honest day's work;

could crush the life out of you
if he cared to
but usually kept to himself

raised Hereford cattle
one summer
to make ends meet.

One had pink eye that never cured.
Dad called him "Popeye"
and paid him special attention.

When time came for slaughter
he soothed Popeye's nerves
with a subdued soliloquy

as he calmly ushered
the hulking steer
into the death chamber restraints

awaiting the captive bolt
stun gun blast to spiral him
into greener pastures.

The local butcher sliced and wrapped
Popeye's innards in wax paper
and delivered to our back porch freezer.

That Spring, I fired up the charcoal,
anticipating the marinated remnants
my mother had prepared.

The family gathered
at the dining table
and having said "Grace",

I observed my father methodically carve
the first piece of meat away from the bone
bloody red juices filling the dinner plate.

He took a bite
and then turned away.

It was the first time
I ever saw my father cry.

Toys in the Attic

From the faraway crawlspace
of attic breeding dust

faint, intermittent cries
cloister in heavy sighs.

Follow their sounds
past boxes of relics—

old board games missing dice
and stuffed animals with severed heads

to broken bookshelves
beneath layers of pink insulation

providing lean-to shelter

seven calico kittens
snuggled, persevering nipples.

The Crow

The crow struts
through the garden
on cornstalk legs
with stick figure feet
and cartoon toes,
angles across hills
of beans and tomatoes,
head bobbing
like foam rubber dice
from a rear view visor,
flexes its black puppet
wings and fluffs its
feathers, appearing
almost to smile,

poses
for a pack
of playing cards.

Small Town Friday Nights in September

They arrive
in a streaming caravan of cars
and big yellow buses plastered
with posters and rainbow graffiti
on roll paper banners.

It is Friday night in September
and the whole town
is huddled at the stadium
under the four towers of light;
air thick with the intoxicating aroma
of chili dogs, hot chocolate
and body odor.

On a field of Bermuda green lined in white chalk,
an enigmatic formation is taking place
with pacman progressions
of brass and woodwinds parting ways
from percussion, snare drums rolling like distant thunder
as they high step off the field
and into the long shadows.

Mascots in animal suits
and cheerleaders in skimpy skirts
blitz the crowd with somersaults, backflips
and other assorted acrobatics
to an approving audience
of bobblehead dolls
as the captains from both teams casually
stroll to midfield to formally introduce themselves
with a coin flip and a handshake.

A moment of silence
as heads bow in prayer
petitioning victory
in the name of Jesus;

prelude to the feeding
of the lions.

Night Sounds (Appalachia, VA)

Syncopation of bedsprings
from apartment next door echoes
steady moan of cars cruising Main
coughing loudly the
coal miner
trembles upstairs
with black lung,
confined
to his sweaty mattress
& his fat wife singing
gospel songs
to the beat
of his despair.

Stray dogs fish
thru silver garbage cans reading
"Keep Virginia Green",
piss on expired meters,
dissatisfied
with the meager find.

Tired, you slip thru the amber fog
of stairwell light,
return to the door
which bears your number,
cubicle of privacy,
borrowed womb;

smell of tonight's table scraps,
cold spaghetti
on the oven, beer bottles

scattered beyond reach
of 2-ply trash bags.
moonlight Sonata
on the stereo

sweet essence
of solitude.

Scottsboro 9

Innocence takes a back seat,
railroaded and cuffed
in an Alabama country courtroom
as Justice paces the hallways
in nervous anticipation.

The stench of Hatred thickens
like burning sulfur
as Justice blindly gropes
through the corridors adjacent
the graying walls of fate.

9 young men stand falsely condemned
by the black bile spewing
from lips of the naked jester
as Justice roams the hallways,
urinating in the drinking fountains.

Ti Jean

Kerouac is dead
& so the generation
that hounded him into his grave
October, 1969.

Hitchhiked across this vast landscape,
discovered the pulse of amerika
& recorded it
on rolls of paper towelling.

Slept in freight cars, adobe,
graying tenements on Haight Street, Chelsea,
typewriter singing jazzy confessions
of a choirboy from Lowell, Massachusetts

in search of the amerikan dream;
found refuge
in skid row visionaries
in basement bar rooms vibrant

with spontaneous nocturnal rhythms
of Bird Parker's saxophone.
On the road
waited six years to be heard,

wrote novels
off the top of his head
from Mexico, Tangiers,
Amerika

never really understood.
Fame brought him nothing,

took to hiding on rooftops
from strangers, friends

drove him
to a small white house

in Florida,
shades drawn, needing whiskey to sleep.

Never quite understood,
loved his freedom--
back yard with a picket fence,
left curious reporters

unraveling question marks
from wild typewritten pages,
disappointed,
found a young man, tired and gray

beyond his years
blandly phrasing
republican politics,
crying over manuscripts.

Role Models

One summer Saturday in 1962
when I was seven years old
and still had heroes,
all my buddies and me were playing baseball
in the front yard and I was Bobby Richardson
covering second base like a natural

when Gary popped one up and laser quick I leapt
beyond the ditch into foul territory (marked by street),
stretched my gloved hand out and smacked the asphalt pavement
cracking open the left side of my head
like a ripe watermelon exploding
from Gallagher's signature sledgehammer

and it wasn't the neighborhood fans screaming
but my mother as she cradled
my head in her hands, thick red blood
soaking into her white silk blouse……….

A few years later, I tried my hand at First,
grew my hair out like Joe Pepitone
and whenever a pop fly drifted my way,
I would watch it spin in the air
until harmlessly dropping into the street,

then casually reach into my shirt pocket,
take out a comb and wave at my mother
who stood looking through the bay window;
this time considerably less exasperated.

Spinning

In a world where objects
in the mirror are closer
than they appear,
vultures descend
upon the sunshine state casting
long dark shadows.

Without flinching,
these charlatans are quick
to unveil the latest martyr,
with the media comfortably
in their hind pockets
like a snakeskin wallet

posting photos in angelic poses
from earlier youth
and painting new skin tones
across the face of his assassin
to make of him
whatever is politically correct at the time;

spinning the same story lines
over and over,
aided by Photoshop edits
and spliced audio files
until you can no longer believe
your own eyes and ears

while the reverent ringmasters
make clowns of us all
and we are left

to consume the entire box
of cracker jacks
only to discover that this time

they forgot to leave
the prize inside.

Hope

The tree trimmers have left
my glorious Maple
botched and butchered,
hat racked and jaded.

The tree is barren now.
The seedlings shocked
from their stems.

Birds and squirrels
refuse to nest here anymore.

Amputated limbs
bare crude replicas
of Flying V guitars, diviner rods
or broken swastikas.

Black bark peels in the sun
like dead skin.

But Spring is near
and the air is pregnant with rain.

Mirage (Nevada Moon)

Egg yolk moon over Nevada
quivers in the smoky mist
of a bloodshot sky.

Neon bleeds like candle wax.
Gold dust radiates from statues,
Glass and sand.

Steady drone
from spinning wheels and show tunes
swells my brain like a cantaloupe.

Hung over, my head is chiseled
full of holes from shots
of Jack Daniels, chinks

of martini glasses, loose
change and the bone rattle
of snake eyes in the pit.

Stars hang in the waning desert sky
like sequin jackets,
moth-eaten and obsolete.

Light and Dark: The Sleeping Forest

After work,
you fill the emptiness
with Jim Beam, hard
whiskey to feed
the slow burn inside..............

The animals come out at night—
feel their hot breath heaving inside you,
pulsing steel curtain eyes,
prowling the dark of your mind,
the headaches that won't go away........

Pumped gas all week
to escape welfare,
mesmerized by the digits spinning
madly into the thousands
for minimum wage;

replay thoughts of the young punk
shoving a Smith & Wesson in your face,
laughing as he circled the pumps, fleeing
into the chaos of the night;
the silver-haired southern bitch
in the gray Eldorado
calling you "boy",

how she cowered when the forest shook,
the skeletal face paled
when the beasts began to stir
behind your angry eyes..............

You rub the nervous scar
branding the stride of your left leg,

shrapnel souvenirs garnered
from a war without heroes—

A number in a fishbowl
stole your future, football
scholarship at Ohio State, Pasadena
in the winter……………

tucked an M-16 in your armpit, grenades
in your deep pockets, then parachuted you
into the crimson tide of an Asian hell.
Jungle sucking your life into its own.

(Barely eighteen
you still remembered
the heroic war stories
your father had told you,
whiskey leaping from his
burning breath, bloodshot eyes
forcing back the pain.
You felt ashamed
by thoughts of desertion.)

You learned to sniff out the enemy,
random flesh clinging to your smelly boots,
idly watching whole villages consumed in flames,
adolescent women screaming over dead husbands,
children twisted beneath charred bicycles
pumped full of American artillery
when they refused to die.

Soldiers slept next to
shot dead from bureaucratic incompetence,

dirty needles, spoiled milk dripping
from desperate veins...............

Back home,
L.A. was in celebration—
Banners held high saluted
The mighty Trojans' Rose Bowl victory
over Ohio State,

called you "Baby Burner"
when you stepped off the plane.

You swallow another shot of whiskey
chased with beer.
Listen to an old Byrds' album, Hendrix
and Stones, reading Kafka by candlelight, drifting..............

Slept in mountains
with no need for weapons,
knew creeks & rivers
by their Cherokee names.
Learned the secrets
of the wilderness,
the divine interplay
between man & Nature,
of light and shadow,
the love of a good woman;
remedy for the memory
of lost souls lurking in that incessant jungle night

(sniper fire ripped clean to bone,
slow motion dreams of gaining turf
for the famed Buckeye backfield
blacked out by a bamboo curtain of blood.)

She never minded the awkward limp,
the fact you couldn't dance
anymore,
good in bed
she always said,
but you felt clumsy,
never in rhythm.....................

She went with the deer,
clash of metal & glass
on a cold rainy night
left her body limp on dark highway....

(Firebombs had leveled the village,
the sick smell of napalm,
engulfing the senses,
left smoking weeks after............)

This whiskey leaves you dizzy,
numb in your empty apartment
listening to the cry of night trains,
staring at dreams in glass frames
gathering dust.

Thoughts turn to the Purple Heart
flushed down a pay toilet in L.A.,
dead corpses piled in a corner,
the women who turned you down.

Cradling an empty liquor bottle,
you stumble across the broken furniture,
hear the muted cheers
greeting you deep into Trojan territory;

the hum of enemy machine fire
cutting you down
inches away from new ground.

Quietly you ease into bed,
full of whiskey to shroud the outcome,
head swimming from the smell of gasoline,
sheets the color of fire;

Coyote eyes spinning wildly
in the smoke-filled room

Lie down with the darkness

so as not to disturb
the sleeping forest.

Popcorn Anyone?

Love has finally come to me
in the form of a deluxe box
of hot buttered popcorn
with an appropriate douche
of salt.

All of the ancient sex goddesses
from my fantasies have materialized
in creamy white morsels curiously sculpted
into the soft mounds
of corseted breasts.

It is intermission of the film classic
"The Blue Angel"
and my tongue maneuvers itself
inside the box as if it were making love
to Miss Marlene Dietrich.

Old Photographs Stare Like Death

Old photographs stare like death
        from the pages of a high school
        yearbook that read as an obituary
                for Youth.

        It is midnight and I am glancing
        through the gallery recalling the faces
        of old friends and past lovers
                and I touch them

        as if I was touching Death.
        I close the book as if
        I were the sealing the lid
                on a coffin.

Big Pockets

Explosion in the Gulf, eleven lives
disintegrate from Deepwater Horizon.

Headlines across America burst into orange
and black mushroom flames.

Fish carcasses and tar balls beach
along the coastlines of five states,

arrive before half-naked tourists converge
to stake claims with lounge chairs and umbrellas.

Billions of dollars spent
for clean-up and oil recovery

Thousands of wildlife lay waste,
designated collateral damage in the oil slick abyss.

Volunteers scrub the survivors
with Dawn detergent.

Meanwhile, one-armed bandits
conduct business as usual,

spinning record breaking profits
from bullet proof glass booths.

Puppet

The instant
of absolute helplessness
when the flash
of revolving lights
appears in the rear view mirror

or when you're lying naked
on the white sanitized tissue
stretched across the green exam table
and the doctor commands you
to roll over on your side,

knees bent, facing the wall
and you comply
like a well-trained dog
followed by the uncomfortable pause,
that blatant hesitation

as if time had suddenly frozen
or this was the day
when the earth actually stood still
until the smack of latex
against the fisted hand

snaps you back to reality
and alerts you to what is coming
yet still you are not prepared
for the lubricating jelly
that feels like cold dog slobber

as you clench your gluteus muscles,
muscles you never realized existed
until this very moment

when you sense that
the very hand of God
has reached up inside you

and it is then you realize

your life is not yours to control;
halfway expect
to hear yourself
speaking in tongues.

Take as Directed

I swallow my speech
with a handful of pills

blood red teeth
wired to deny

silence is a dagger
to the heart’s frail fabric

it only hurts
when I smile.

Metamorphosis

Without love
you labor
through the long slow nights,

voices you cherish
yet never hear
whisper through woodwork,

chill the spine
of ships buried at sea;
crushed from the gravity

of indifference
and the sounds
of lies;

cockroach gripped
to the braille
of tiles,

conscious
of the algebra
of footsteps.

Last Dance

The sky gradually blackens
as an oil spill quietly consuming ocean.
Sparrows plummet from air,
litter the lawn like buckshot.

Cicadas broadcast
their haunting vuvuzelas
from the decaying hearts
of evergreens.

Plagued by the rust of world events,
my soul is a highway sign
peppered with bullet holes.

A North wind rips thru pines,
crying like a cat in heat.
The branches' blistered fingertips
strum twisted guitar chords played backwards.

Gypsy moths circle the driveway,
their powdered wings dizzy from the dance
cling to the yellow moonbeams
of floodlights set to introduce the unsteady rise

of exhaust fumes swirling
from beneath the steel garage door

a reluctant apparition
on opening night.

The Absolution of July

Despite firecracker heat,
transparently
like a passionate whisper,
tomatoes on the vine
bursting with red.

Bullets and Baseball

It was a bullet
off the bat
of Mark McGuire
that rifled just over
the left field wall
of Busch Stadium
in 1998
that eclipsed Roger Maris's
Home Run mark
recorded back in '61
before the advent
of andro, HGH & steroid cocktails;
before the Boys of Summer traded
a true love of the game
for the insatiable greed
of collective bargaining;
back when starry-eyed little kids
like me
still had heroes.

It was a shot
that accomplished
what most bullets aspire to,
eradicating that
which is pure,
innocent & natural

and that which
will never be seen again
in this lifetime.

Big Stone Gap, The Early Years

Town carved from a valley of pines
spread before the magnificent
expanse of Powell Mountain

Pennsylvania speculators
settled here nearly a century
ago, modern day pilgrims
with dreams of dollars,
clutching charters,

wrestled mineral rights
from simple mountain folk
with fistfuls of dollars
like a prime rib dangling
before the mongrel dog.....

Now another day assumes
the winding caravan,
journey through Andover past
rows of company houses, the

one familiar tenement trembling
alongside railroad tracks with
"Praise God Anyhow"
lettered in yellow spray paint.

The trains that kept you
awake last night still
firing black smoke
at the dawn.

Stonega / Osaka
thick with early morning mist.

Watching the Men Lay Cable through the Neighborhood

Two white guys
& a black guy
in white hard hats
stand in a semi-circle
sucking on cigarettes and chatting
on 2-way radios.

Three Spanish guys,
from the waist up,
shoveling feverishly.

Windowpane

I see hungry moths feasting
on street lamps, yellow globes
wired with spider silk,
filaments of moon, closet
of dreams.

I see gnarled pine trees rooted
in charred ground, branches furled
in quiet submission, withered arms
offering swastikas
of surrender.

I see emblazoned
upon cellophane glass, full moon's
cold accusing eye watching me
watch young lovers
writhing in the long shadows.

I see a velvet cape stretched spandex
over drum filled with black water;
a hungry black spider kiting the rafters,
its spiny fingers spooling
a fine silk blade shrouding
these long hot summer nights.

I see a butane ocean of sky
surging with the bitter grief
of loved ones,
my own grief held back
by the chewed gristle of the heart.

Spiders and stipple
winged moths hunger, circling about
in clouds like a spray of bullets
from gunmetal cylinder roulette,
spray of shattered moonlit glass;

spores of light
scraped
from the drowning
flame
of a warm suicide.

Rendezvous

Blue
replaces the fog

comes into me
my one lover

moves thru my life
like a revolving door

in and out
in and out

and finally
exhausted,

drifts like
tired smoke

leaves me
still my one friend,

not slamming the door
as she left.

Why They Decided to Use Canaries

The chatty parrot
in the coal mine
had captured everyone's
complete attention
while telling a dirty joke,
eliciting bright smiles
on the blackened faces
of hard working men
but just before
he got
to the punchline

Homage to Mr. Wizard

Velcro gripped
to the schoolyard playground
I lie sprawled

in grass-stained, knee-patched
blue denim jeans.

A crowd gathers
as prisms of sunlight

take aim thru my pocket-sized
magnifying glass

dissolving brown brittle leaves
into wisps of smoke;

my friends' faces
like fish on a stringer,
astonished and amazed.

May 9, 2010

The trees renew
their tapestries of green
and the playful chatter
of gray squirrels returns.

Maple seedlings
complete their curious
whirlybird descent.

The vegetable garden's
black earth has softened, bursting
with flowering tomatoes
and sprawling cucumber vines.

With each measured strike
of true temper hoe, I sense
my father's forearms and hands
torqued and flexing
alongside my own;

The lilac bush
parades purple corsages
clusters clinging tenuously
fragile memories of past springs.

Sky blue eggs
nestled in English boxwood
splinter into transparent
baby robins

their heads tilted back
to take in first breath

just as my father's
to take in his last.

Fishing Wallen's Creek

Anchored to a moss-covered boulder,
Beneath a procrastinating sun,
Pace of a dog's lazy eye.

Refrain of locusts
Strums from high chaparrals,
Thick with goldenrods
& blue thistle.

Canadian geese sweep the perimeter.
Cacophony of crows
In the distance, chainsaw
Reverberating throughout the canyon,
Chewing up wet pines.

Stench of chain oil,
Smoldering campfires linger
On the tongue
Like stale cigarettes.

Flannel shirt snagged by barbed wire,
Eyes burning sweat and
Grit in the teeth, fingertips bloodied
From bait hooks;

Yet I am drawn
To the scrolling waters,
Trout lancing the teal complacency;
Leaping in the corrugated surf,

Arc of rainbow reels
Beneath the rippling stream
Spinning circles
In the maelstrom,

Finally to succumb
To the compelling pull of destiny—

Four pound test
of a Zebco 33.

Snowglobe

Snowflakes pirouette
like figurines on silver ice skates
gliding effortlessly across a glacial pond
fronting a candy coated Victorian castle adorned
with sparkling lights and golden bells and green
wreathes tied with little red ribbons
as children with perfect smiles
dance and sway and sing and play, frolicking
around plump white snowmen
in such a wonderful
carefree world
just before
the earth shook.

Stick Horse

On my fifth birthday
My mother drew one of my father's socks
From the dresser drawer,
Stuffed it with old yellowing handkerchiefs,
Sketched large enchanting eyes
With a magic marker
And tied it securely to the end
Of a broken broom handle
That was just my size, then clipped
The fringe of an old rug
To fashion a mane and stapled
A loop of rope
Into the painted wood
To make for me a stick horse
And constant companion
That me,
Not knowing any better,
Simply thought
Was something
That mothers do.

LIFE

With a smirk
she slid three tiles
onto the bottom right corner
of the board
to spell
ZOO

triple word score, 36 points……..

Taking the sand glass timer
down to the final grain,
I manage to utilize five tiles

from my rack connecting
with the word "tic"
to create
ECLECTIC

a grand total of eleven points
for my efforts…………….

Art
imitating Game
imitating
Life.

Still Life from a High School Parking Lot (1972)

Three faceless figures
With oil stained baseball caps
Worn backwards
Leaning under the hood
Of a 1965 Ford Mustang.

The Eleventh Month

In the chill of receding twilight
we manipulate swirls
of fallen leaves.

Gold, saffron, scarlet red
& amber crackle
like small campfires gathered

in the metronome sweeps
exposing frame
after frame
of forest green grass.

A thin veil of gray cirrus
drapes the Maryland landscape
as pumpkin tinged sun
extends its ephemeral rays

dissipating like fine silk
into distant smoke
of horizon.

I pause to contemplate
the light of another day
drawing to a close

and the comforting cloak
that is infinite darkness
closing in.

About the Author

Ben Rasnic is a native of Jonesville, a small rural town in Southwest Virginia with a population <1000. His poems have been published in *A Small Good Magazine*, *Bird's Eye reView*, *The Camel Review*, *Camroc Press Review*, *Flutter Magazine*, *Gutter Eloquence*, *The Orange Room Review*, *Right Hand Pointing*, *The Rusty Truck*, *Short, Fast and Deadly*, *Subliminal Interiors*, *Victorian Velvet Press* and numerous other print and online journals. He is also the author of "Artifacts and Legends", a chapbook collection of poetry from Aldrich Press and "The Day the Looking Glass Shattered" an e-chapbook from The Camel Saloon. A Pushcart Prize nominee in 2011, Rasnic still considers as his greatest literary achievement, electing to publish two short poems by Yusef Komunyakaa while serving as editor of his college literary magazine, Jimson Weed, in 1978—16 years before Komunyakaa received the Pulitzer Prize for Poetry. Ben currently resides in Bowie, Maryland.

Made in the USA
Las Vegas, NV
13 October 2024

96755084R00056